Granny Marmalade
and Uncle Tractor

written by
Julian Warrender

illustrated by
Gavin Rowe

For your free copy of the Granny Marmalade and Uncle Tractor song go to www.hareandheronpress.com.

"This charming book takes children on a journey through the farming year in the company of Granny Marmalade and Uncle Tractor. The author's enthusiasm for food is infectious and will no doubt encourage children to take an interest in what they eat and where it comes from."

– Ronda Armitage, children's author

Oh, it is glorious being a Granny!

This book is for my family, who fill my heart with joy.
With huge respect, love and thanks to Gavin Rowe, Carlotta Luke,
Dorothy Stannard and Paul Austin Kelly, for their assorted and amazing talents,
generous contributions and their encouragement and belief in this project.
My thanks also go to the OV ladies for their support and interest –
A, A, A, C, E, J, M, C, T & T – what a team!
And finally a special thank you to Uncle Tractor
for agricultural advice and loyal enthusiasm.

Published by Hare & Heron Press 2013
14 Court Road, Lewes
East Sussex BN7 2SA
www.hareandheronpress.com

Written by Julian Warrender
Illustrated by Gavin Rowe
Designed and produced by Carlotta Luke
Edited by Dorothy Stannard
The Granny Marmalade song written and composed by Paul Austin Kelly
Hare & Heron Press logo designed and drawn by James Otway

A percentage of the profits from this book will be donated to Dandelion Time, www.dandeliontime.org.uk

Copyright © Julian Warrender 2013
ISBN: 978-0-9574730-0-3

Printed by Manor Creative Ltd using vegetable-based ink on FSC accredited paper

FSC MIX Paper from responsible sources FSC® C018405

Introduction

THIS BOOK IS BASED ON TWO REAL PEOPLE – the author Julian Warrender (Granny Marmalade) and her son (Uncle Tractor). Julian started her 'jam factory', Ouse Valley Foods, from the cottage where she lived with her son Jamie, who is a farmer.

The idea to turn her experiences into a children's book came about after Julian's other son, Joseph, had a child, and she became a grandmother and Jamie an uncle; you can guess the nicknames they were given! Julian's aim is to illustrate the symbiotic, timeless relationship between food, cooking and farming and to capture the delights and challenges of life on the farm through the seasons, the joys of growing fruit and vegetables, the fun of responsible foraging, and the sticky pleasure of making marmalade – excitements that her grandson Jasper loves to share.

Granny Marmalade

GRANNY MARMALADE HAS A JAM FACTORY full of huge shiny saucepans, a fridge as big as a garden shed, hundreds and hundreds of jam jars, and lots and lots of brown sacks full of sugar, spices and silky flour.

Her factory is in a large, wooden-framed barn next door to the old farmhouse, which she shares with her son, Uncle Tractor. Just up the lane lives her friendly little grandson Jasper.

There is always music and laughter in Granny Marmalade's busy kitchen. All year round she can be found creating delectable concoctions – sweet sticky jams, wibbly-wobbly jellies, spicy scented chutneys and, of course, her famous marmalade.

When cooking, Granny Marmalade likes to wear dungarees, stripy socks and a brightly coloured scarf to wrap up her long, long hair.

and Uncle Tractor

UNCLE TRACTOR HAS A GINORMOUS RED TRACTOR with tyres that weigh as much as 10 elephants and an engine as loud as a dragon's roar. All year round he tends to the land and cares for the animals on the farm. He has big, bristly pink pigs, black-faced sheep and a herd of pedigree cattle. Granny Marmalade has a flock of hens and an enormous cockerel called Cecil. Jasper has two pet ducks called Pesto and Nutmeg.

Uncle Tractor is proud of his powerful tractor. In the cab is a fridge, where he hides his lunch, and a radio that keeps him company.

Uncle Tractor wears work clothes; he has seven pairs of blue overalls, one for each day of the week, and thick, warm socks that Granny Marmalade knitted for him.

January

GRANNY MARMALADE LOVES JANUARY. Big wooden crates of Seville oranges from sunny Spain, glossy Sicilian lemons and tight-skinned tangerines from Tangier are delivered to the kitchen for her to turn into delicious marmalades.

In her warm, fragrant kitchen, she cuts, chops and juices huge piles of fruit, and boils it up in big steaming pans. Just the right amount of sugar is added to this murky brew, which bubbles and burps until glossy and thick. Last of all, she pours it into shiny glass jars, ready to be bought by marmalade lovers from Sussex to Siberia.

On the dark evenings, Granny Marmalade repairs the scarecrow that keeps the birds from eating the fruit and vegetables in the kitchen garden. She dresses it in a pair of Uncle Tractor's old overalls stuffed with straw, a hat she found at a jumble sale and a pair of dark glasses! Jasper has named the scarecrow Bert.

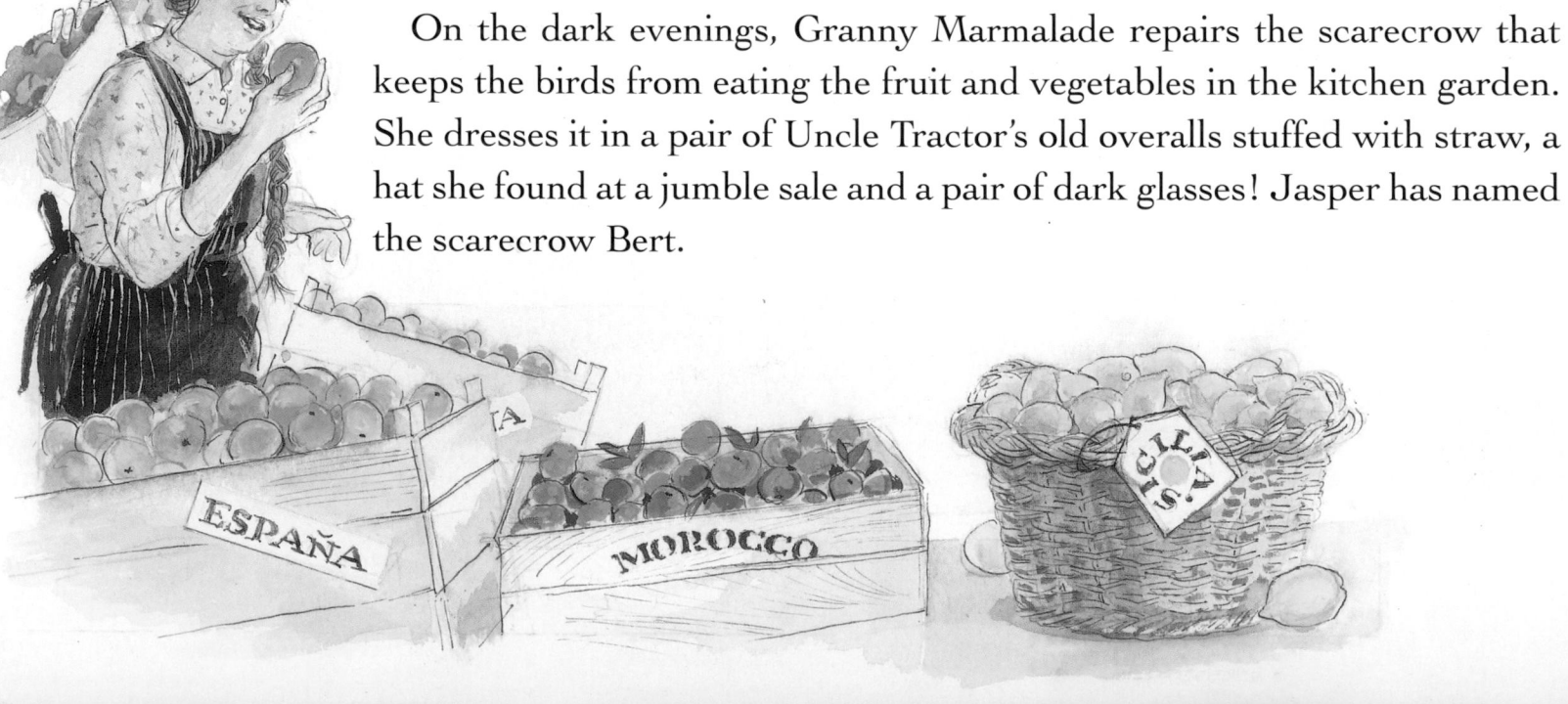

Hurrah, it's marmalade time again!

-An American breakfast idea: toast a muffin and spread with butter and orange marmalade. Top with very crispy, streaky bacon.

-Good on a really cold winter's day as a pudding: steamed vanilla sponge with warmed marmalade poured over the top (perhaps custard, too).

January

UNCLE TRACTOR LOVES MARMALADE. He has it for breakfast on thick slices of toast before he goes off to work. Uncle Tractor doesn't like January. On some mornings he would prefer to stay in bed under his snug duvet! He puts on two pairs of socks, a woolly hat and great big gum boots before getting into his tractor. He turns the radio on to check the forecast and puts the heater on to keep his feet warm.

Winter is a harsh time for Uncle Tractor's animals. The cold makes them hungrier than ever. When the fields are bare of grass and too wet and soggy for the cows to graze, Uncle Tractor has the never-ending job of bringing them sweet hay or steamy, smelly silage to eat in the shelter of their cosy byre. He also does lots of hedge-cutting, before the birds arrive to build their nests in spring. Sometimes, when the snow clogs the lanes, Uncle Tractor rescues the cars that get stuck. He tows them out of trouble with his powerful tractor and helps the grateful drivers on their way.

February

ON DARK, DANK DAYS when there is not much jam to prepare, Granny Marmalade loves making soup. She uses knobbly, bobbly Jerusalem artichokes and sturdy leeks that have weathered the winter underground, in a corner of the vegetable patch. Artichokes are at their sweetest at this time of the year, and Granny Marmalade transforms them into delicious soup to sell at the farmers' market.

If there is enough left over, she fills a flask for Uncle Tractor to take for his lunch. She cooks the soup in a big cauldron that hubble-bubbles on the hob; she stirs it with a wooden spoon that is at least a metre long.

Some February thoughts
-An interesting addition to a bowl of soup: cut stale bread into small cubes, toss in an equal mix of olive oil and soy sauce, spread out on a baking tray and toast in the oven till they turn brown and crispy.
-Ah, pancakes! Good fillings: lemon and lavender marmalade; cinnamon and pears; chocolate and orange curd.

Pancake time comes round again and lemons are at their peak. Granny Marmalade loves to have fun flip-flopping pancakes in a big, flat, sizzling frying pan and then smothering them with sugar and shivery lemon juice.

For a change, she crams them with warmed jam made from pears that have been carefully stashed away in the cool, dark cellar since last autumn. Granny Marmalade makes smooth, silky curd out of the lemons that are left over. She keeps a pot for herself and Jasper to eat straight from the jar when no one is looking!

February

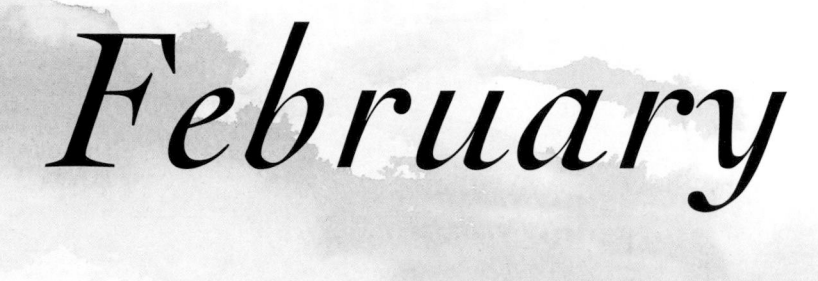

UNCLE TRACTOR HAS LOTS MORE TO FINISH before the spring brings a flurry of new season's activity on the farm. Now is the time to sow the seed for this year's harvest. Beans are planted in regimental rows on the sunny-sided, south-facing slopes; the flat, fertile fields are for spring wheat.

On some days, Uncle Tractor takes the silver-bladed plough and carves deep furrows in the cold, compacted soil; he loves to see the seagulls wheeling and circling in the sky behind the tractor, gobbling up the worms turned up by his plough. By the end of each long, long day he likes to take off his gum boots and warm himself in front of the crackling fire!

March

GRANNY MARMALADE BEGINS TO PREPARE for a busy time in her kitchen. Chirrupy birdsong wakes her up early, the days have lengthened and spring is around the corner.

If the weather is mild, by the end of March spiky wild garlic covers the riverbanks with a scented carpet of fresh green leaves and starry white flowers. Granny Marmalade makes the most delicious pesto from wild garlic.

<u>March meals</u>
-Pesto is perfect with pasta, stirred into risotto, dolloped onto minestrone soup or spread on toasted ciabatta with melting mozzarella.

-In Italy, they say that the water pasta is cooked in should be as salty as the sea. Pasta is cooked if it will stick to the wall when thrown at it!

Slender stems of rose-pink rhubarb have also pushed their way into the world; hidden from view during the chilly winter, they are now ready to be made into the year's first batch of jam.

As a treat for hungry Uncle Tractor when he comes home, Granny Marmalade cooks rhubarb tucked under crunchy crumble; for an extra special treat, she serves it with cream provided by the cows on the farm.

March

ON THE FARM, NEW LIVES ARE BEGINNING. The barn is full of the urgent, soft sound of bleating lambs. Most of the sheep have twins. Occasionally Granny Marmalade helps Uncle Tractor deliver triplets. The lambs, still unsteady on their legs, stay close to their mothers in the safe, warm shelter until they are strong enough to skip and gambol in the meadows.

When it is too wet to get out into the fields, Uncle Tractor tinkers around in the workshop, mending the farm machinery. Jasper loves to come and watch. On days when Uncle Tractor is not too busy, he lets Jasper sit beside him in the tractor cab.

Now is the time to make sure the tractors, forage harvester and other equipment are in working order. The enormous green combine is primed ready for the harvest; later in the year it will be in the fields working day and night.

April

THE VEGETABLE GARDEN NEEDS DIGGING in preparation for planting summer crops. Granny Marmalade grows loads of striped courgettes for her chutneys, and at least three varieties of tomatoes in her greenhouse. She will sow fuzzy-blue cornflowers and golden marigolds between the rows of vegetables and stand Bert the Scarecrow among the lettuces to keep the pigeons from eating the tender seedlings.

If the weather is warm and spring starts early, the first clusters of elderflower appear around the edges of the fields and alongside the lanes. Twirly-whirly hop fronds are beginning to twist and turn through the hedgerows and the sun starts its steady climb towards midsummer heights.

Granny Marmalade and her little whitish dog Poppy love to go for early morning walks and pick the first lacy-headed blossoms to infuse her jams and jellies with their fragrant scent.

Elderflower ideas
Elderflower cordial (only pick what is necessary for the recipe, in order to be thoughtful towards the countryside): steep 2 handfuls of blossom heads in a litre of hot water with 3 sliced lemons and 3 teaspoons citric acid; leave for 2 days; strain, heat, stir in 1kg granulated sugar. Bottle and keep in fridge. Can be used to flavour ice cream, cakes & fruit salads.

April

AS THE DAYS BEGIN TO LENGTHEN, Uncle Tractor gets up a little earlier so he can get through the increasing demands on the farm. The chickens must be let out of their ark; Cecil the Cockerel has been crowing encouragement for the day to unfold since the first shaft of spring sunshine pierced the horizon.

April showers have helped the lush, spring grass to shoot up, and Uncle Tractor trundles up and down the fields with his heavy, clanky roller, levelling out the deep ruts. The weeds need taming; they will strangle the grass unless Uncle Tractor gets there first and nips them off with the topper.

By now the sheep and cattle have been liberated from their winter quarters. Before the day is done, Uncle Tractor takes Jasper down to the meadows alongside the river to check that the ewes and their lambs are safe and contented.

May

MAY IS AN EXCITING, BUSTLY, BUSY TIME in Granny Marmalade's kitchen. Her friend David grows the best asparagus in the whole wide world. He has been carefully watching for the first signs of this mysterious plant to peep above the soil. Asparagus appears secretly, under the cover of mild spring nights, and can grow up to 15 centimetres by daybreak!

David and his team of helpers use special sharp-bladed knives to cut the plump spears off at ground level, before placing them carefully in shallow wicker baskets, ready to be tied in bundles to sell in his busy farm shop.

Granny Marmalade has been getting ready to make pots and pots and pots of rich, buttery hollandaise sauce to guzzle with the tender green asparagus spears. By mid-June, when the asparagus season ends, she will have used 300 kilos of salty butter and 5,000 freshly laid hens' eggs!

Granny Marmalade and her team of cooks have been waiting patiently for the new season's produce; the kitchen is now aglow with brightly coloured vegetables – handsome purple aubergines, marble-sized cherry tomatoes and plump green peppers are turned into tasty chutneys and hot, tongue-tingling pickles.

IRISH CREAMERY BUTTER

May

UNCLE TRACTOR HAS LONG, HARD-WORKING DAYS ahead of him, so every morning he makes himself an enormous packed lunch. He likes sandwiches made from a big, billowy white loaf, cut into hunks that are at least eight centimetres deep and bulging with cheese and Granny Marmalade's pickle. Afterwards he has two large wedges of cake filled with raspberry jam.

The fields sway with grass that is so long it reaches the top of Uncle Tractor's gum boots. It is time for him and his friend Grant to make tons and tons of silage.

They set off at the crack of dawn and do not get back until night has fallen. The men take it in turns to drive the forager. As the grass cascades out of the shoot, it is collected in the trailer. The silage is piled up into mountainous heaps and then covered with tarpaulins to mature into a pungent winter feast for the cows.

Now the daytime has lengthened, the chickens lay eggs every day; they have free range of the yard, so Granny Marmalade asks Jasper to help hunt for their well-hidden nests. She is clever at knowing where to look and may find as many as 24. She sells them to passersby at the farm gate.

June

AT LAST GRANNY MARMALADE SEES THE EFFORTS of her hard work and patience sprouting in the vegetable garden. Finger-sized cucumbers peep from under prickly leaves, radishes swell to rosy globes, and beans dangle downwards as the sun rises higher.

Granny Marmalade has netted the strawberry bed and raspberry canes to protect the fruit from pecking birds and nibbling mice. Jasper loves picking strawberries and popping the juiciest ones into his mouth before Granny Marmalade misses them!

June is a month of celebrations: Granny Marmalade and Uncle Tractor have birthdays. They invite all their favourite people to a picnic by the river. Granny Marmalade bakes a cake three layers deep, crammed with jam and crusty clotted cream. Uncle Tractor decorates his tractor and trailer with streamers and bunches of flowers; he helps Granny Marmalade, their happy friends, family and Poppy into the trailer and everyone trundles to the meadow for the fun and games.

Happy Birthday!

June is birthday month
...for the picnic...
-Raspberry Jam Tarts:
roll puff pastry,
line tart tins with
pastry, half fill with
raspberry jam, bake
for 8 mins.
-Spicy Sausage rolls:
mix a good dollop
of pickle or chutney
into the sausage meat
before sealing into
pastry.

June

WARM SUMMER DAYS MEAN HOT SHEEP! It is time for Uncle Tractor to shear his flock of woolly ewes. The clippers clatter as the fleeces are shorn, revealing soft and creamy summer coats. The sheep are impatient for their turn to be over, so they can wriggle free and return to the fields.

It is the height of the hay-making season and the air is filled with the sweet aroma of crushed meadow grass; Uncle Tractor needs extra help on the farm during the busy summer months. The men and women work long hours, late into the evenings.

Granny Marmalade brings the hard-working, hungry team a jug of refreshing lemonade, clinking with ice, and a basket of peppery pork pies and cold sausages.

July

THE ABUNDANCE OF FRUIT AND VEGETABLES keeps Granny Marmalade and her team in the kitchen as busy as bees all day long. Great big vats of chutneys hubble-bubble; ladies chatter and chop; hundreds of jars are filled with an array of summer bounty. Shiny cherries, downy peaches, and berries like precious jewels are tumbled into pans with sugar, to be transformed into jams and preserves.

In front of the farmhouse is a towering mulberry tree over 150 years old. The fruit is now ripe. Granny Marmalade wears her oldest pair of dungarees and wraps her long plaited hair under a scarf. It is messy work; the squishy purple fruit bursts as it is picked and the juice runs down her arms.

The mulberries are used for making into a jelly, which Granny Marmalade will give to her friends at Christmas.

July fruit ideas
-Smoothie suggestions:
"Berry Burst" - raspberries,
strawberries, mint and lemonade
"A Currant Affair" - black, white
and red currants, lemonade
"Peaches & Cream" - peaches,
vanilla ice cream, lemonade

When the summer evenings are light, and the nights sprinkled with stars, Granny Marmalade and Jasper sleep in a tepee that Uncle Tractor gave her for her birthday. They love to listen to the scuffle and snuffle of badgers in their night-time foraging and the tweeting and twittering of the birds in the early morning.

July

IT IS THE TIME OF THE YEAR for the biggest machine on the farm to come out of its shed. The colossal combine harvester thunders into action, with Uncle Tractor in the cab; he must work all day, and long into the balmy summer nights. On some evenings, he gives Granny Marmalade and Poppy a ride, and Granny Marmalade takes over from Uncle Tractor if he needs a rest.

The first field to be harvested is planted with oilseed rape. The glowing yellow flowers of spring are now dark seed heads, which will be turned into a golden, glossy oil, perfect for frying chips in!

On rainy days, Uncle Tractor prepares his cattle for the summer agricultural show. He shampoos their coats, clips and oils their hooves, and curls their tails. Uncle Tractor takes great pride in his animals and has won many prizes.

August holiday ideas
Some unusual mixes
for the ice cream
maker; experiment with
fruit (and veg!):
-Greengage and
home-made honeycomb
-Melon and basil
-Cherries and toasted
flaked almonds
-Cucumber and mint

August

GRANNY MARMALADE LOVES CLIMBING TREES. She has an orchard heavy with fruit. Greengages ripen first. Granny Marmalade and her tall friend Ruth get the long ladder and baskets; they take it in turns to hold the steps and climb to the tops of the trees, where the best fruit has been warmed by the sun. Jasper and his friends, William, Henry and Freddy, play in the orchard while Granny Marmalade and Ruth fill the baskets to the brim. They pick 64 kilos, which are then mixed with honey to make a special conserve for Granny Marmalade's very best customers.

In the vegetable garden, the cucumbers and the first of the onions are ready for pickling. Granny Marmalade makes crunchy relishes, which she stores in a dark cupboard ready for the Christmas hampers.

When it is too hot in the kitchen, Granny Marmalade has a peaceful snooze in the shade of the old mulberry tree, with her shoes off, and Poppy fast asleep under her stripy deck chair.

August

EVERYONE ON THE FARM IS EXHAUSTED but pleased with the results of their hard work. The grain silo is full to the brim with wheat. The barn is crammed with straw; this will be used as cosy bedding for the cattle on cold winter nights.

The hens and bossy Cecil the Cockerel are enjoying an unexpected meal – little heaps of corn spilt in the yard by the trailers. Uncle Tractor will sell the grain and soon large cumbersome lorries will rattle down the lane to collect the bounty.

Before the autumn showers set in, Uncle Tractor takes the forage harvester out to cut the grass one last time. This is the last haul of silage for the year; it will be used to feed the cows through the long, dark months ahead.

When the wind is in the right direction and the days are damp, Uncle Tractor muck-spreads. His steamy, pongy load is spread on the fields to encourage the grass to grow thick and lush next year. Granny Marmalade does not hang the washing out on those days!

September

AS THE DAYS GROW SHORTER and the weather nippier, high in the sky, above the woods, inky-black rooks helter-skelter downwards in the restless gusts of wind. Granny Marmalade, Jasper and Poppy are off foraging. The hedgerows are crammed full of berries and other wild treats; hard crab apples, musky elderberries, flame-coloured rosehips and glossy blackberries hang on the branches ready to be picked.

In the kitchen, the ladies are excited to see the booty! They get to work, turning the berries into highly prized jellies, sharply spiked with the tang of autumn.

Wheelbarrows full of beetroots, swedes the size of footballs, and enormous stripy marrows arrive at the kitchen door; Granny Marmalade has been growing these specially for the Harvest Festival. Everyone on the farm joins in the celebration, held in the old Sussex barn when the moon is at its fullest; they laugh and are merry, drink punch and dance jigs to the tunes on an old violin.

September - back to school month
A hedgerow recipe: Blackberry, Bramley
and Elderberry crumble
Rough-cut peeled Bramley apples
and mix with two-thirds blackberries and
one-third elderberries. Add a little sugar.
Top with crumble made with wholemeal flour,
butter, demerara sugar and ground hedgerow
hazelnuts.

September

UNCLE TRACTOR NEEDS TO HARVEST the rest of his crops. The swishing swathes of maize stand at least two metres tall. Each majestic plant has four or five plump ears bursting with glossy, yellow kernels of corn. The crop is gathered and turned into winter feed for the cattle.

He also has to lift the potatoes and sugar beet; if the frost comes before he can gather the vegetables, they will turn to mush underground.

Once the last of the harvest is in, the fields are drilled and rolled. Winter barley, oats and wheat are planted to exactly the right depth, in straight rows, ensuring an even growth by next spring.

It is time for the annual Ploughing Match. All the farmers come with their tractors and massive heavy horses, some with funny little scruffy dogs in their cabs; they compete to plough straight, even furrows and the winner goes home with a big silver trophy. Uncle Tractor has won the cup five times – once more than Granny Marmalade!

October - toffee apple
time
Take a medium-sized
sweet apple such as Cox
or Spartan, skewer a
lollipop stick through
the centre, starting at
the stalk end. Make a
toffee mix with butter
and brown sugar. Dip
the apple into it,
covering the whole
fruit. Place on
greaseproof paper till
hardened.

October

BOUGHS ARE HEAVY WITH APPLES now plumped up and ready for picking. Granny Marmalade loves picking apples; she gently puts the fruit in baskets, careful not to bruise them. Most are placed in cold storage, where they will keep for nearly seven months. In Granny Marmalade's kitchen they use 5,000 kilos of apples a year to make into hundreds and hundreds of jars of chutneys, jams and jellies.

The sloe bushes that edge the riverbanks are also in fruit. As winter bites, the birds will eat the bitter berries. Granny Marmalade picks them to make a special tipple called sloe gin that Uncle Tractor and their friends will have on New Year's Eve.

Granny Marmalade and Jasper get up early to gather the mushrooms that grow in the far corner of the orchard; it is a special place that only a few people know about.

Uncle Tractor scrambles freshly laid hens' eggs, picks the last few tomatoes in the greenhouse, grills crispy bacon and fries the pink-gilled mushrooms to make a special breakfast feast for himself and Granny Marmalade.

October

TIME HAS COME FOR UNCLE TRACTOR'S SHEEP to have their annual dip to rid them of nasty creepy-crawlies. The sheep do not like being soaked, so Uncle Tractor has to encourage them to leap in and out of the water. Jasper laughs with excitement to see such a sight!

On market day, Uncle Tractor drives to town in the horse box. The farm needs a new young bull for his breeding herd of pedigree cows. Uncle Tractor enjoys the hustle and bustle of the livestock market and the babble of the auctioneer; he likes to meet up with his fellow farmers and chat about the price of wheat and the cost of lambs. While in town, Uncle Tractor buys himself a new pair of blue overalls and a pair of green gum boots.

Back at the farm, the last of the apples in the orchard have fallen to the ground; gusty autumn winds rattle the branches and dislodge the fruit. Uncle Tractor lets loose the greedy pigs to gobble up the fermenting apples. There is a terrible din, as the oinking, grunting beasts push and shove to get there first!

November

TENDER VEGETABLES NO LONGER GROW in the kitchen garden; frost crusts the plants that are left, and only the hardy cauliflower and sprouts flourish. Granny Marmalade makes piccalilli from the cauliflower; it is a favourite of Uncle Tractor's; he will eat it with slices of ham for his supper.

Some kind friends have brought baskets full of quinces to the kitchen. They have a tree in their garden that is as old as Granny Marmalade. The golden yellow fruit are chopped, boiled and strained to release a fragrant juice, and then boiled with sugar to make a crystal-clear, amber jelly.

It is Stir up Sunday this month, the traditional day to make the Christmas pud. Everyone gathers in the kitchen to help stir the gloopy mixture; Granny Marmalade makes sure that a good glug of brandy goes in, while Jasper puts the last handful of currants into the bowl. The pudding is shaped to the size of a football and then wrapped in white muslin to await a good boiling on Christmas Day.

November - time to think of the birds
Fat balls: keep a bit of the Christmas
pud back. Mix pud with softened lard
and form into spheres. Push the ends
of a loop of string into the ball for
hanging off branches in the garden.

November

UNCLE TRACTOR SPENDS some of the bright cold days of winter checking that the farm buildings are watertight and the gutters free from autumn leaves. He must make sure the cows are warm and draught-free in the barn; if they get cold they might get ill and Uncle Tractor does not want to call out the vet in the middle of the night. If any of the cows are due to calf he must take special care of them. After the calf is born its mother will be able to produce milk for 300 days!

The sheep are happy to remain outside in the bleak, bare fields; they have thick woolly fleeces to keep them warm. If there is snow on the ground, Uncle Tractor feeds them extra rations of sweet sugar beet, sheep nuts and hay.

December

GRANNY MARMALADE IS FRANTICALLY BUSY with orders for Christmas. Trays of purple figs and scratchy-skinned pineapples arrive from the fruit market and the tantalising aroma of spices, oranges and dried fruit wafts from the kitchen: she is making her very secret recipe for Mince Meat. Granny Marmalade and her team make 500 jars to sell at the last farmers' market of the year.

There is a terrific air of excitement at the Jam Factory as Christmas draws nearer; crisp, crunchy, pickled red cabbage, boozy brandy butter and scarlet cranberry sauce have to be prepared in time for the feast.

By Christmas Eve the kitchen is silent; the very last jar has been filled, the noisy clatter of machines has stopped, the aprons have been hung up, and the hard-working team have gone home for a well-earned break.

The farmhouse will soon be filled with happy noise, jolly laughter, barky dogs and excited children; but before the celebrations begin, Granny Marmalade has one last thing to do… she wraps up an enormous mountain of presents in bright, shiny paper and coloured, curly ribbon; she is especially careful to tuck Jasper's gift behind the twinkling Christmas tree…

December - present ideas
-Mince pies with pastry initial on top
-Cranberry sauce in pretty little glass jars
-Shortbread Christmas tree decorations
-Chocolate and orange truffles

December

THE YEAR IS NEARLY AT AN END, though work continues for Uncle Tractor. He has some very special tasks to complete before Christmas Day. The households in the nearby villages need spiky, red-berried holly to decorate their homes and sprigs of mistletoe to kiss under! He fills the trailer full of branches and bunches and goes from house to house selling the seasonal greenery.

On Christmas Eve, he checks his animals are fed and contented, and shuts the chickens in their ark, safe from the cunning fox. It is only when all is well on the farm that Uncle Tractor can take off his muddy boots, fold up his overalls and join Granny Marmalade for the fun and festivities…

…not forgetting to hang his Christmas stocking at the end of his bed!

Recipes

AN INTENSELY ORANGEY MARMALADE
FOR ADULTS TO MAKE

This marmalade can be made at any time of the year, using a variety of sharp oranges depending on what is in season.

Personally, I love using minneolas, a cross between a tangerine and a grapefruit that has a delicious, intense flavour, no pips, thin skins and a brilliant deep orange colour. The season for minneolas is at its height in February and March.

Another fun variety to use are blood oranges; the very best flavoured, Arancia Rossa di Sicilia, come from the slopes of Mount Etna in Sicily and are available from January to March. The distinctive, deep, burnished-red flesh develops when low night-time temperatures are followed by warm sunny days.

The following recipe should make a year's supply for a family of four!

2.3kg of oranges or minneolas
1kg of lemons
5.4ltr of water
5.5kg of granulated sugar

METHOD
• Quarter the oranges and lemons.
• Remove any pips.
• Finely slice fruit – approximately 2mm.
• Soak sliced fruit in the water for at least 12 hours.
• The next day, put water and fruit in a pan twice the capacity of the contents. Bring to the boil with lid on. When it reaches boiling point, turn down heat and gently simmer for 2½ hours with lid just propped open.
• When cooking is complete, add all the sugar, being sure to stir in thoroughly.
• At this point, the mix needs to be cooked in approximately 2.2ltr batches in a traditional open jam pan. To do this, decant 2.2ltr into the jam pan.
• Boil rapidly for 5 mins and then turn heat down to a steady rolling boil. Cook for 10 mins.
• Remove from heat and rest for 5–10 mins.
• Return to heat and boil until mixture is thickening, glossy and going "blurp, blurp". (I find tests with thermometers, saucers, etc., to be far less effective than the look and sound of the boiling mix!!)
• Remove from heat and leave to stand for 10 mins.
• Pot in sterilised jars and lid them immediately.
• Repeat the last eight steps with the rest of the mix.

Marmalade should be stored away from direct sunlight, in a cool area. It will keep pretty well indefinitely though the texture will thicken and the colour darken if left for more than 18 months.

JASPER'S ORANGE AND MANDARIN
NEARLY MARMALADE

Here is a recipe that will introduce young taste buds to the deliciousness of marmalade. It can be made from start to finish by an eager five-year-old!

2 135g packets of orange jelly
2 295g tins of mandarin segments in fruit juice
2 medium-sized oranges

METHOD
• Remove the zest from the two oranges, taking care to make the shreds as long as possible. Use a special citrus zester to do this.
• Put zest to one side.
• Cut oranges in half and squeeze; keep the juice.
• Drain the mandarins, keeping the juice.

• Combine the mandarin and orange juice and measure. You will need 570ml. If there is not enough juice, make up the difference with water.
• Cut the jelly into squares and combine with the juice mix.
• Warm jelly and juice in the microwave, then stir the mix until the jelly dissolves.
• Allow to become tepid.
• Add mandarin pieces and orange zest.
• Allow mix to cool until it begins to thicken and the shreds are suspended.
• Pour the mix into clean jam jars and lid them immediately.
• Place in the fridge to complete setting process.
• Store in the fridge.